L'ART ET INSTRUCTION
DE BIEN DANCER

L'ART ET INSTRUCTION
DE BIEN DANCER

(MICHEL TOULOUZE, PARIS)

MUSIC TRANSCRIBED AND EDITED BY
RICHARD RASTALL M.A.Mus.B. Ph.D.

TRANSLATED BY Dr. A. E. LEQUET

The Noverre Press

This edition published in 2022 by
The Noverre Press
Southwold House
Isington Road
Binsted
Hampshire
GU34 4PH

ISBN 978-1-914311-37-6

© 2022 The Noverre Press

LART ET INSTRUCTION
DE BIEN DANCER
(MICHEL TOULOUZE, PARIS)

A FACSIMILE OF THE ONLY RECORDED COPY
WITH A BIBLIOGRAPHICAL NOTE BY
VICTOR SCHOLDERER

PRINTED FOR
THE ROYAL COLLEGE OF PHYSICIANS
OF LONDON 1936

BIBLIOGRAPHICAL NOTE

The anonymous book here reproduced, *L'art d'instruction de bien dancer*, can probably claim to be the first printed book extant which is devoted to the art, or pastime, of dancing. To the best of the present writer's knowledge, the only evidence of an earlier one is the assertion by an Italian authority of the eighteenth century that the *Ballarino perfetto* of one Rinaldo Rigoni was printed at Milan in the year 1468. But this very early date conflicts with the received opinion that printing was not introduced into Milan until 1471, both author and title are unknown to the standard bibliographies and no copy of any such book is forthcoming to-day. The *Art et instruction* thus holds the field, and it will always remain an interesting and early representative of its species, even if some future lucky find should oust it from pride of first place.

The copy from which the reproduction has been taken is unique, so far as we know, and has never been adequately described. It appears to have come into the possession of its present owners, the Royal College of Physicians of London, as part of a munificent bequest of some three thousand books made to the College by Henry

Pierrepoint, first Marquis of Dorchester, who died in 1680, but it contains no positive indications of provenance whatever. On a fly-leaf at the beginning is written the title "Instruction de bien dancer". This is followed by the title-leaf of a rare French tract of the year 1494, "La noble et excellente entree Du Roy nostre sire en la ville de florence qui fut le xvii.e. Iour de nouembre. cccc.iiii.xx ᵼ xiiii", with a woodcut representing the King's entry; it is touched up with pen-and-ink and has the words: "Imprime en Paris en annº dñi: mº ccccº: lxxxviij" written beneath. Then comes a leaf with more manuscript, headed "The præface to yᵉ Reader:" and beginning:

The dilligence that oʳ forfathers have alwaies
vside to plesure there posterite as it doth apeare
manye wayes: so doth yt also in this Instruction
of ther fately and modeste manere of dācinge

and ending at the foot of the page with a reference to "Erasmus the fownder of newfāglidnes", who "ys nowe lyttelle sette by". The purpose of this preface (which is presumably made up for the occasion) and of the other additions is obscure. Beneath the colophon of the *Art et instruction* itself is written in large figures "1488:" a date about which there will be more to say presently. The binding is modern.

Michel Toulouze, of Paris, the printer of the *Art et instruction*, is known to have set his name to rather more than a dozen very tolerably printed quartos, none of great length and all but one undated. Their interest for us is concentrated in the four of their number which secure for Toulouze a mention among the early printers of music, namely, the *Art et instruction* itself, two editions of the *Musicales regulae* of Guillaume Guerson de Longueville (or Villelongue) and an edition of the same author's *Missae solemniores*. These all contain musical notes printed from movable type on a four-line stave. Guerson was a musician of repute and his *Musicales regulae*, a treatise on the elements of music, plain-chant, counterpoint and other matters, was still being reprinted as late as 1550; the editions of Toulouze are in all probability the first and second. He was likewise a bookseller and, in a very small way, a publisher; in one of his colophons he gives notice that at his shop on Mont Sainte-Geneviève there may be found a singing master (presumably himself) with his music-books, prepared to instruct any likely lad in all points of his art "with a jovial countenance". He died shortly before 31 January 1502/3, and the document which gives us this information also mentions Toulouze as owing him a sum of money at the time. Although several of Guerson's little tracts describe themselves as actually printed by him, their typographical connection with Toulouze is so close as to make it probable that they were really commissioned at his press by Guerson. One of them, a selection of Christmas carols for the use of a sisterhood of penitents, entitled *Noels tres excelens*, is not only printed with the same large type as the *Art et instruction* but also contains the very same border-piece of a snail distracted by the simultaneous onset of two angry birds before and behind which appears on the fifth page of the *Art*. This, with its side-pieces and the two small ornaments of the colophon, evidently derives from a book of Hours or some similar publication, not now traceable. Guerson's name is absent from the *Art et instruction*, but it is hard to believe that Toulouze would have put such a text in hand without his cognizance and allowance.

It is impossible to feel sure of the date of the *Art et instruction*. Of the material employed in it only the admirably decorative bird-and-beast capital at the beginning can be linked to precise dates, the set to which it belongs having been in use in 1496, 1499 and 1501. The woodcut of a lady and gentleman on the last page occurs in a its worn state in an edition of the romance of *Paris et Vienne* printed by Denis Meslier about 1490 and was probably made for this in the first instance, its suitability to other contexts causing it to be retained for further use. The watermarks, an eight-rayed star and what appears to be a pyx or reliquary on a tall stem, are not very distinctive. More helpful is the mention of Toulouze's address in the colophon as at the sign of the Hart's Horn (in the Clos Bruneau) on Mont Saint-Hilaire, for one of the five known books bearing his address, Guerson's *Missae solemniores*, contains a large device with the printer's monogram which is found again, recut and considerably altered, in at least two books issued at the sign of St. John the Evangelist in the Rue des Amandiers. As we know from a notarial record that Toulouze moved into the latter premises on 30 December, 1496, it follows that everything which he printed at the Hart's Horn must be earlier than this. Exactly how much earlier is, however, an open question. One printed date does indeed occur in the group, and that is 15 November, 1482, at the end of a law-student's compendium by one Hieronymus Clarius. Unfortunately, this book also contains printed initials, a refinement which was apparently not introduced into Parisian incunabula until several years later than 1482, so that the day specified is probably that on which the author, not the printer, completed his task. Still more unfortunately, the date 1488 already mentioned as written at the end of the *Art et instruction* itself (but not included in the reproduction) is condemned by the authorities in the Department of Manuscripts at the British Museum, who consider it to be very much later than the fifteenth century and probably from the same hand as the title and "præface" at the beginning. Yet the date is both impressively precise and quite acceptable in itself and the suggestion may perhaps be hazarded that it derives from a genuinely contemporary note of purchase or ownership which was written on a fly-leaf now destroyed. On this guess we must be content to leave the matter.

V.S.

REFERENCES

The *Ballarino perfetto* of 1468 is mentioned in the preface of Giambattista Dufort's *Trattato del ballo nobile* (1728). Rigoni is a shadowy figure; was his true date perhaps 1648? It is a fact, however, that dancing was all the rage at the Milanese court in the 1460's. Antonio Cornazzano wrote a dance-book for one of the court ladies in 1465; it is still extant in manuscript but there is no evidence that it was ever printed, although several of its author's other writings were put into type during the 1470's.

The remainder of the Note is founded upon the sections dealing with Toulouze and Guerson in the second volume of A. Claudin's *Histoire de l'imprimerie en France au xve et xvie siècle*. A copy of the presumable first edition of Guerson's *musicales regulae* forms part of the exhibit of early music printing in the British Museum, where it has hitherto been dated 'about 1505'. The other edition signed by Toulouze and his edition of the *missae solemniores* are described in M. L. Polain's *catalogue de livres imprimés au quinzième siècle des bibliothèques de Belgique*, nos. 1763 and 1764. The woodcut from Meslier's edition of *Paris et Vienne* is reproduced on p. 110 of the second volume of Claudin's above mentioned work.

SELECT BIBLIOGRAPHY

Much work has been done on the Basse Dance since the foregoing Note and References were written. For further information on "L'art et instruction de bien dancer", its repertory and notation, and the performance of Basse Dances, see the following:

Bukofzer, Manfred: "A Polyphonic Bass Dance of the Renaissance" in *Studies in Medieval and Renaissance Music* (New York, 1950)

Dean Smith, Margaret: "A Fifteenth Century Dancing Book" in *Journal of the English Folk Dance and Song Society* III (1937)

Dolmetsch, Mabel: *Dances of England and France from 1450 to 1600* (London, 1949)

Heartz, Daniel: "The Basse Dance. Its Evolution circa 1450 to 1550" in *Annales musicologiques* VI (1958-63)

——————: "A 15th-Century Ballo: *Rôti Bouilli Joyeux*" in *Aspects of Medieval and Renaissance Music: a birthday offering to Gustave Reese*, ed. Jan LaRue (London, 1967)

——————: "Hoftanz and Basse Dance" in *Journal of the American Musicological Society* XIX (1966)

Jackman, James L.: *Fifteenth Century Basse Dances* (Wellesley College, 1964)

Kinkeldey, Otto: "Dance Tunes of the Fifteenth Century" in *Instrumental Music*, ed. David G. Hughes (Cambridge, Mass., 1959).

NOTE ON THE TRANSCRIPTION

In transcribing "L'art et instruction de bien dancer" (hereafter referred to as T) one cannot ignore a closely-related source of the Basse dance repertory, the beautiful contemporary MS which is now MS 9085 in the Royal Library at Brussels (hereafter, B). These two sources do not always give identical readings in the 43 tunes that are common to them, and neither source is perfect: but in some cases where T's text is obviously faulty, B gives an acceptable reading. This transcription therefore owes much to James L. Jackman's collation of the two sources (see Select Bibliography). Margaret Dean Smith's article provides more information on the Brussels MS and the circumstances of T's publication.

T's notation for the dance-steps is retained, except that R is used throughout for the opening reverence, where T often uses r (his sign for a *démarche*, or *reprise*). Where the choreography is defective, additional steps are supplied to complete the dance. I have not, however, supplied steps for those sections of nos. 20 and 21 where choreography is lacking altogether: these and no. 19 present too many problems that cannot yet be solved satisfactorily. Each *mesure* in the transcription is marked off by an oblique stroke.

The unmeasured tunes are notated in semibreves, but where T gives a final long I have used a *fermata*. The measured *pas de Bréban* are transcribed in 6/8 time, which is less confusing to the eye than is 6/4: it should not be taken to imply too fast a speed.

All accidentals are editorial suggestions. Other editorial additions are enclosed in brackets [ ]. An obelisk (†) indicates a correction to T's text: the nature of such an alteration can be seen by comparing the transcription with the facsimile. An asterisk (*) indicates a correction, addition or omission for which B gives authority: an asterisk between notes on the stave shows the pitch of an omitted note. All other information is footnoted.

January 1971

Richard Rastall
University of Leeds

Sensuit lart et instruction de bien dancer.

Pour lart et instruction de dācer basse dance Il est a noter que basse dance tout premieremēt se diuise en trois pties Cest ascauoir en grāt mesure ē moyenne z en petite mesure

La grand mesure pour entree de basse dance se doit marchier par vne desmarche puis p vug brāle puis par .ii. pas siples puis p. v. doubles puis p. ii. pas siples comme deuāt puis .з. desmarches z puis fault fayre vug brāle. La moyenne mesure se doit faire marcher par .ii. pas simples puis p з. pas doubles puis par .ii. siples puis par .з. desmarches et fault faire vug branle.

La petite mesure se doit cōmēcer amarchier p ii pas siples puis p i pas double puis p ii siples puis p з desmarches z puis fault ferze .i. b

Cest a scauoyr q̄ .ii. pas siples. i pas double vne desmarche z vug brāle ocupent autant de tēps vug cōme lautre. Cest adire q̄ chescum deux doit ocuper vne note entiere de

A.i

There follows the art and instruction of good dancing.

For the art and instruction of dancing the *basse danse*, it should be noted to begin with that the *basse danse* is divided into three parts. That is to say, into "grand measure", "medium" and "little measure".

The "grand measure" for the entry of the *basse danse* must be trodden with one *démarche*, then with a *branle*, then with 2 single paces, then with 5 double paces, then with 2 single paces as before, then with 3 *démarches*, and then you must do a *branle*.

The "medium measure" must be trodden with 2 single paces, then with 3 double paces, then with 2 single paces, then with 3 *démarches* and then you must do a *branle*.

The "little measure" must begin by 2 single paces, followed by a double pace, then by 2 single paces, then by 3 *démarches* and then you must do a *branle*.

Remember that 2 single paces, one double pace, one *démarche* and one *branle* are all of the same duration. That is to say each one of them should last one whole note of the *basse*

basse dāce cest assauoir .ii. pas si ples oibuēt ocuper vne note vug pas double vne note vne desmarche vne note et pareillement vug brā=le vne note.

ET en ses choses ycy est la basse dance vraye et acōplie du tout. Note q̄ toute basse dance se comāce par desmarche et se fine par brāle. Et se nōme basse dance pour ce q̄ on la ioue selon maieur parfayt et pour ce q̄ quant on la dance on va en pays sās soy deme-ner le plus gracieusemēt q̄ on peult. Item est a noter quil ya deux manieres de basse dance Cest assauoyr basse dance maieur et basse dāce mineur Basse dance maieur ce cōmence par basse dance Et pour la premiere note que est nōmee desmarche on fayt reuerēce a la fāme en soy enclināt vers elle et ceste enclinacion ce doibt fayre du pie senestre.

BAsse dance mineur ce cōmance p̄ pas de barban et de la premiere note on ne fait point de reuerence a la fāme. Item pour au vray danser vne basse dance deux choses sont req̄ses p̄mierement que on saiche le nōbre de pas dune checune basse dance Et secondemēt q̄ on les saiche marcher par bōne mesure. Si

danse, namely, 2 single paces should last one note, one double pace one note, one *démarche* one note and similarly one *branle* one note.

Thus is the *basse danse* truly correct in every detail. Note that every *basse danse* begins by a *démarche* and ends with a *branle*. And it is called the *basse danse* because it is played according to the major perfect and because it is danced serenely without gesticulation and as gracefully as possible. Note also that there are two kinds of *basse danse,* namely the *basse danse majeure* and the *basse danse mineure*. The *basse danse majeure* begins by a *basse danse* and for the first note which is called *démarche,* one bows to the lady, bending towards her, and this should be done with the left foot.

The *basse danse mineure* begins with a *pas de Brabant,* and on the first note, one does not bow to the lady. In order to dance correctly the *basse danse,* two things are required, firstly that one should know the number of paces in each *basse danse,* and secondly that one should know how to tread them according to the correct measure. It is thus necessary to

fault & est de necessité de monstrer & enseigner
la maniere cōment on doibt marcher.

ET p̄mieremēt. Une desmarche seulle
se doibt fayre du pie destre en reculāt et
sa pelle desmarche pour ce que on recule et se
doibt fayre en éclinant son corps et reculer le
pie dextre pres de l'autre pie.

Le secunde desmarche se doibt fayre du pie
senestre en éclināt son corps pareillemēt & soy
tourner vug petit devers la fāme puis a me
ner le pie dextre en pres du senestre en clināt
son corps pareillemēt. La tierce se doibt fayre du pie dextre cōme la premiere.

Le branle se doibt cōmencer du pie senestre
et se doibt finer du pie dextre & s'apelle branle
pource q̄ on le fayt en brālāt d'ūg pie sur l'au-

Les deux pas siples se font en auant & /tre
le p̄mier pas siple se fayt du pie senestre en
enclināt son corps & fayre vug pas auant.

Et le segōt pas simple se fayt du pie dextre
et fault elever son corps & marcher vūg petit
auant. Le p̄mier pas double se fayt d'u pie
senestre & fault elever son corps & marcher .ʒ.
pas en auant legierement. Le segond pas
double se doibt fayre du pie dextre & fault pa-
Au

how and to teach the way one must tread.

Firstly, a single *démarche* must be made with the right foot in retreating, and it is called *démarche* because one retreats, and it must be made with an inclination of the body and bringing the right foot back near to the other.

The second *démarche* must be made with the left foot with a similar inclination of the body, turning slightly towards the lady, then bringing the right foot near to the left one with one more inclination of the body. The third should be made with the right foot like the first.

The *branle* should start with the left foot and end with the right foot, and it is called the *branle* because it is done by swaying from one foot onto the other. The two single paces are made in advancing and the first single pace is made with the left foot, inclining the body, and taking a pace forward. And the second single pace is made with the left foot, raising the body and moving forward slightly. The first double pace is made with the left foot, raising the body and taking 3 paces forward lightly. The second double pace is made with the right

rellemēt eleuer son cōrps τ puis marcher .ƺ.
pas eu auāt le p̄mier du pie dextre. le segōd
du senestre τ le tiers du dextre. ¶ e tierspa
double se doibt fayre du pie senestre cōme l̄
p̄mier. Le quart pas double se doibt fayre dt
dextre comme le segond. Et le quit se doibt
fayre du pie senextre cōme le p̄mier τ le tiers

Ꝋtem est a scauoyr q̄ iamais il nia qu
ti. pas siples en seble selō lart de biē dā-
Item est a sauoyr q̄ les pas doubles sōt/ cet
tousiours nō p̄ selō lart de bien dācer aubra⸗
Note q̄ quāt on fayt deux pas siples apres
le pas double on doibt fayre le p̄mier du pie
dextre τ le segond du pie senestre affin que on
face la p̄miere desmarche du pie dextre cōme
dessus est dist. Item il ya vne regle gn̄ale
en toutes basses danses que tout p̄mieremēt
onfayt vne desmarche τ puis fault fayre bug
brāle τ puis. ii. pas siples τ puis les pas dou⸗
bles τ puis. ii. pas simples si la mesure de la
basse danse le reqert τ puis les desmarches τ
puis le branle. Item il est a noter que au⸗
chune foys on fayt vne desmarche τ auchu⸗
ne fōys trois. Item il est a noter quil ya
auchunes mesures des basses dāses q̄ sōt par

foot and one must likewise raise one's body, then take 3 paces forward, the first with the right foot, the second with the left and the third with the right. The third double pace should be made with the left foot like the first. The fourth should be made with the right like the second. And the fifth with the left foot like the first and the third.

One should also remember that there are never more than 2 single paces together according to the art of good dancing. And again that the double paces are always in uneven numbers according to the right art of good dancing. Note that when taking two single paces after the double pace, one should make the first with the right foot and the second with the left so that the first *démarche* can be made with the right foot as is said above. There is also a general rule in all *basses danses* that first of all one should make one *démarche,* then a *branle,* then 2 single paces, then the double paces, then 2 single paces, if the measure of the *basse danse* requires it, then the *démarches,* and then the *branle.* One should also note that sometimes one makes one *démarche* and sometimes three. Note also that there are some measures of *basse danse*

faytes les autres plus que perfaytes τ les au
tres sont imperfaytes.　　Les mesures per
faytes sont seles qui ont pas simples deuant
les pas doubles et apres auec troys desmarches et vng branle.　　Les autres se disent
plusque perfaytes et sont celes qui ont pas
simples deuant les pas doubles et apres auec
vne desmarche et vng branle.　　Les autres
sont apelees imperfaytes qui ont pas sīples
deuāt les pas doubles τ nout point apres auec
troys desmarches et vng branle.
Et est anoter que pour plus facillement en
tendre les lettres que sen suyuent apres les
notes que pour.R.tu doibs entendre desmar
che pour.B.branle pour.S.pas simple et
pour.D.tu doibs entendre pas double.

hich are perfect, some more than perfect and
thers imperfect. The perfect measures are
those which have single paces before and after
the double paces, followed by three *démarches*
and one *branle*. The others are called more
than perfect and are those which have single
paces before and after the double paces, followed by one *démarche* and one *branle*. The
others, called imperfect, have single paces
before but not after the double paces, followed by three *démarches* and one *branle*.

And one should note that in order to understand more easily the letters that follow after
the notes, for R one should understand
démarche, for B *branle,* for S single pace and
for D double pace.

January 1971

E. Lequet
University of London

Le petit Rouen   In 40 notes and 5 measures as shown

R b ss d d d d d r r r b/ss d r r r b/ss

d d d r r r b/ss d r r r b/ss d d d r r r b

Filles a marier   In 32 notes and †4 measures

R b ss d d d ss r r r b/ss d r r r b/ss d d

d ss r r r b/ss d r r r b

Ma maistresse   In 42 notes and 5 measures

R b ss d d d d d r r r b/ss d r r r b/

ss d d d d d r r r b/ss d r r r b/ss d d d r r r b

Le hault & bas   In 32 notes and 4 measures

R b ss d d d ss r r r b/ss d ss r r r b/ss d

d d r r r b/ss d r r r b

Le moys de may   In 34 notes and 4 measures

R b ss d d d ss r r r b/ss d ss r r r b/ss

d d d ss r r r b/ss d ss r r r b

Triste playsir

In 42 notes and 5 measures

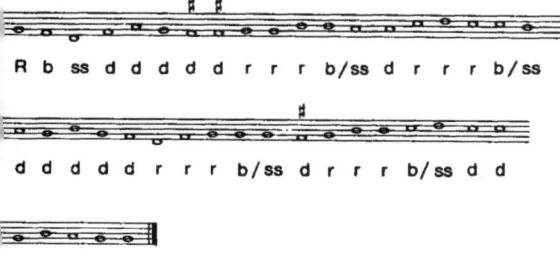

R b ss d d d d d r r r b/ss d r r r b/ss

d d d d d r r r b/ss d r r r b/ss d d

d r r r b

La poytevine

In 44 notes and 5 measures as shown

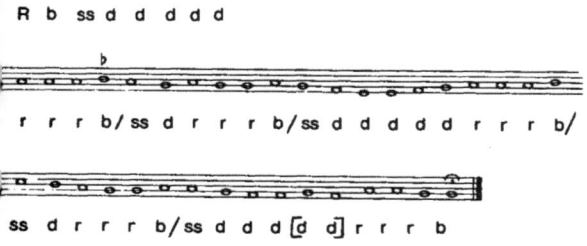

R b ss d d d d d

r r r b/ss d r r r b/ss d d d d d r r r b/

ss d r r r b/ss d d d [d d] r r r b

8. Langueur en nul soit destresse

In 36 notes and 4 measures as shown

R b ss d d d d d ss r r b/ss d d d r r r

b/ss d ss r r r b/ss d d d r r r b

9. Le ioyeulx espoyr[1]

In 2̇2 notes and a *demie* and 3 measures and a *demie*

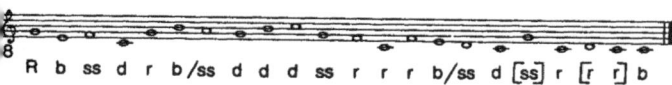

R b ss d r b/ss d d d ss r r r b/ss d [ss] r [r r] b

10. Casulle la novele[2]

In 46 notes and 5 measures as shown

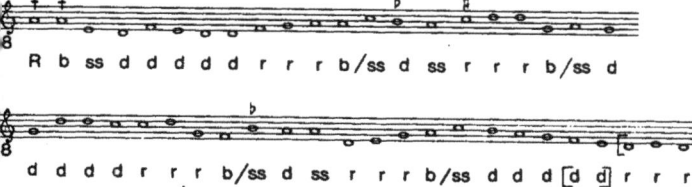

R b ss d d d d d r r r b/ss d ss r r r b/ss d

d d d d r r r b/ss d ss r r r b/ss d d d [d d] r r r b

(1) c.f. no. 34. Daniel Heartz (in " The Basse Dance. Its Evolution...") established that this is the first part of the dance, the "demie" being the triple-time *basse dance mineure* that would follow.

(2) Not in B. The first two notes are corrected, and the last four supplied, from Antonio Cornazzano's version: my accidentals follow the same source. Cornazzano's tune (called "Tenore del Re di Spagna") is in Otto Kinkeldey, "Dance Tunes of the Fifteenth Century".

11. Torin — In 46 notes and 5 measures

R b ss d d d d d ss r r r b/ss d ss r r r b/ss d d

d d d ss r r r b/ss d ss r r r [b]/ss d d d r r r b

12. Le grand roysin — In 42 notes and 5 measures

R b ss d d d d d r r r b/ss d r r r b/ss d d d

d d r r r b/ss d r r [r] b$^{(3)}$/[ss] d d d r r r b

13. Avignon — In 44 notes and 6 measures

R b ss d d d ♯r r r b/ss d r d r b/ss d d d r r r b/

---

(3) Inverted.

ss*d r d r b/ss d d d r r r b/ss d r d r b

4. Je languis In 44 notes and 5 measures

R b ss d d d d d r r r b/ss d ss r r r b/ss d d d

d d r r r b/ss d ss [r] r r b/ss d d d r r r b

5. Le petit roysin In 32 notes and 4 measures

R b ss d d d ss r r r b/ss d*r r r

b/ss d d d ss r r r b/ss d r d r b

16. Ma myeux aymeye In 30 notes and $\overset{\dagger}{3}$ measures

R b ss d r ss d d d ss r r r b/ss d ss*r r r [b]/ss d d d ss

r r r b

17. Le grant thorin In 48 notes and 5 measures

R b ss d d d d d r r r b/ss d d d r r r b/ss d

d d d d r r r b/ss d d d r r r b/ss d d d d d r r r b

18. Ma doulce amour In $\overset{\dagger}{40}$ notes and 4 measures as shown

R b ss d d d d d ss r r r b/ss d d d r r r b/ss d

d d d d ss r r r b/ss d d d r r r b

LA beaulte de castille ce dance a troys per
ss d honeur. d ssd honeur. d ss
tonages de la maniere que sensuit.
honeur d ss ddd ꝛ b ss d ꝛ b ss d.

ROti bolli toieulx lome ⁊ la fame en sen
ble doibuet fayre em pas de braban ⁊ ce
cetí.ii.foys ⁊ puis sensuit la bace doibt fayre
.ii.foys dance

LOme et la fame / lome fait ceti tout seul
lome ⁊ la fame font ceti en sanble et puis la
fame apres vne foys toute soule ⁊ lome ii foys

9. La beaulte de castille[4]

This dance for three people in the manner following

10. Roti bolli ioieulx[6]

The man and the lady together must do a *pas de Brabant* twice, and then follows the *basse dance*.

he man and the lady together once: the man dances his alone, and then the lady alone: then the man and he lady together twice.

[] No satisfactory transcription is possible of the three dances in measured notation (nos. 19, 20 and 21), even by reference to other sources: the transcriptions given here keep as closely as possible to the 15th-century meaning of the notation, although the notation itself is faulty.

[] These groups of four s-q are corrected from B.

[] On the structure and notation of this piece, see Daniel Heartz, "A 15th-Century Ballo: *Rôti Bouilli Joyeux*". The instructions for this dance and the next are so confused that an accurate interpretation is impossible: B's instructions are followed as closely as possible here.

¶ L'Esperance de bourbon en pas de bar
bain et ce dance deux   foys et puis r ci

bayse la fame et puis l'ome et la fame font cet
ensemble   ¶ Sensuit la basse dance.

L'esperace de bourbõ a rbii n. ii m
b ſſ ddd ſſ m b ſſ d T m ʒ b

Aliot nouelle a rrrvi notes a . iiii . M.
ʒ b ſſ d ddddd ſſ m b ſſ ddd m b ſſ d ſſ m

b ſſ ddd m b

1. Lesperance de bourbon

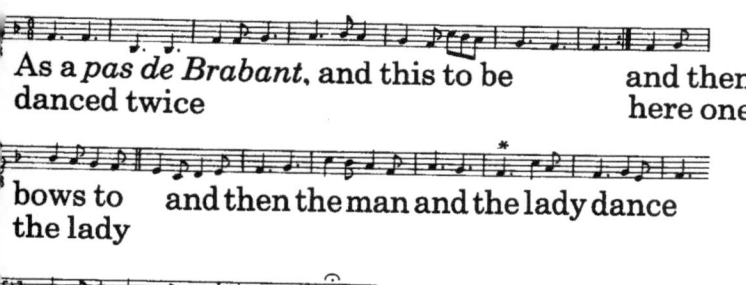

As a *pas de Brabant*, and this to be danced twice
and then here one bows to the lady
and then the man and the lady dance this together.

The *basse dance* follows In 17 notes and 2 measures

b ss d d d ss r r r b/ss d ss r r r b

2. Aliot novelle   In 36 notes and 4 measures

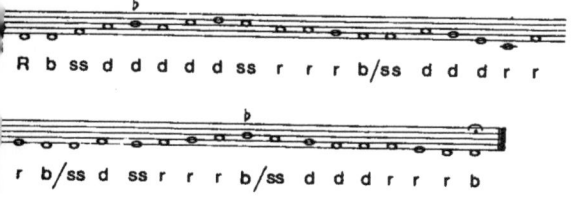

R b ss d d d d d ss r r r b/ss d d d r r

r b/ss d ss r r r b/ss d d d r r r b

La basse dance du roy a xlviii notes a
R 2 b ɾſ ɔɔɔɔɔɯɯ bɾſ ɔɔɔ ɯɯb ɾſɔɔɔɔɔ

mesures.
ɯɯ.b ɾſ ɔɔɔ ɯɯ b ɾſ ɔɔɔɔɔ ɯɯ b

Espoyr a lxii notes a. v. mesures tou-
R 2 b ɾſ ɔɔɔɔɔ ɾſ ɯɯ b ɾſ ɔɔɔ ɾſ ɯɯ b ɾſ

tes parfaytes
ɔɔɔɔɔ ɾſ 2 b ɾſ ɔɔɔ ɾſ ɯɯ b ɾſ ɔɔɔɔɔ ɾſ

ɯɯ b ɾſ ɔɔɔ ɾſ ɯɯ b

Bii

23. La basse dance du roy

In 48 notes and 5 measures

R b ss d d d d d r r r b/ss d d d r r r b/ss

d d d d d r r r b/ss d d d r r r b/ss d d d d d r r r b

24. Lespoyr

In 62 notes and 6̇ measures, all perfect

R b ss d d d d d ss r r r b/ss d d d ss r r

r b/ss d d d d d ss r [r r] b/ss d d d ss

r r r b/ss d d d d d ss r r r b/ss d d d ss r r r b

5. Beaulte[7]   In 39 notes and 4 measures

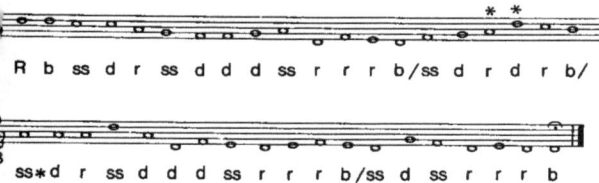

R b ss d r ss d d d ss r r r b/ss d r d r b/

ss*d r ss d d d ss r r r b/ss d ss r r r b

6. Ma mie   In 31 notes and 4 measures

R b ss d d d r r r b/ss d r d r

b/ss d d d r r r b/ss d ss r r r b

7. La verdelete[8]   In 42 notes and 5 measures

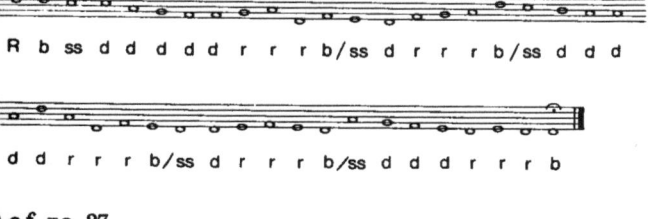

R b ss d d d d d r r r b/ss d r r r b/ss d d d

d d r r r b/ss d r r r b/ss d d d r r r b

c.f. no. 27.

c.f. no. 25.

Les Joyeulx de brucelles a xxxiiii. notes
R bſſ ꝺꝺꝺꝺꝺ ꝫ b ſſ ꝺ ſſ ꝫ b ſſ ꝺꝺꝺ
ſſ ꝫ b ſſ ꝺ ſſ ꝫ b

engolesme a xxxv. notes a. iiii. mesures
R b ſſ ꝺ z ſſ ꝺꝺꝺ ſſ ꝫ b ſſ ꝺ ꝫ b ſſ
ꝺꝺꝺ ſſ ꝫ b ſſ ꝺ ꝫ b]

La belle a xxxi. note a. iiii. mesures
R. b ſſ ꝺꝺꝺ ꝫ b ſſ ꝺ ꝫ b ſſ ꝺꝺꝺ ꝫ b ſſ ꝺ ſſ ꝫ b
B iii

28. Le Joyeulx de brucelles[9]

In 34 notes and 4 measures

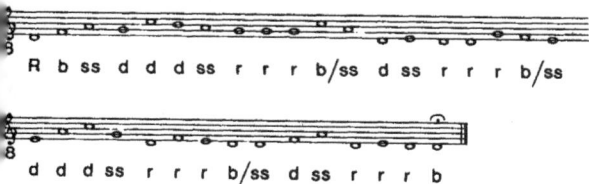

R b ss d d d ss r r r b/ss d ss r r r b/ss

d d d ss r r r b/ss d ss r r r b

29. Engolesme

In 35 notes and 4 measures

R b ss d r ss d d d ss r r r b/ss d r r r

b/ss d d d ss r r r b/ss d r r r b

30. La belle

In 31 notes and 4 measures

R b ss d d d r r r b/ss d r r r b/

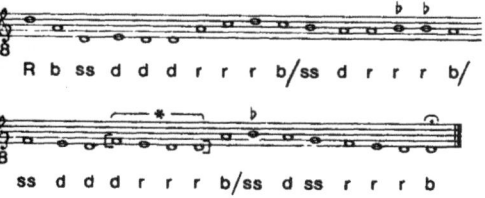

ss d d d r r r b/ss d ss r r r b

[9] The choreography has one step too many. The choreography from B, which is identical to T's after the first *mesure*, is used in this transcription.

31. Bayonne

In 33 notes and 4 measures

R b ss d d d ss r r r b/ss d ss r r r b/ss d d d ss r r r

b/ss d r r r b

32. La navaroyse

In 32 notes and 4 measures

R b ss d d d ss r r r [b]/ss d r d r

b/ss d d d ss r r r b/ss d r d r b

33. Barcelone

In 34 notes and 4 measures

R b ss d d d ss r r r b/ss d ss r r r b/ss d

d d ss r r r b/ss d ss r r r b

4. Florentine[10]   In 44 notes and 5 measures

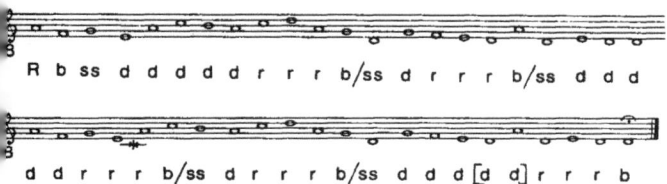

R b ss d d d d d r r r b/ss d r r r b/ss d d d

d d r r r b/ss d r r r b/ss d d d [d d] r r r b

5. La tantayne   In 36 notes and 4 measures

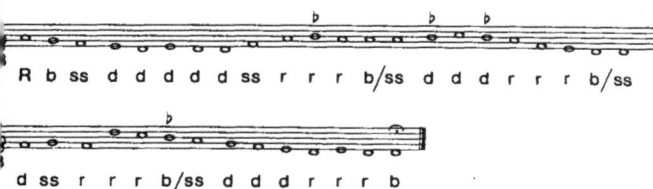

R b ss d d d d d ss r r r b/ss d d d r r r b/ss

d ss r r r b/ss d d d r r r b

6. Barbesieux   In 37 notes and 4 measures

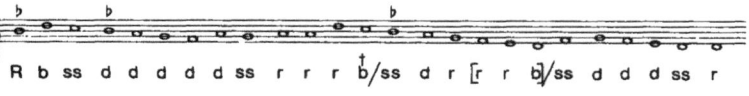

R b ss d d d d d ss r r r b/ss d r [r r b/ss d d d ss r

10) c.f. no. 9.

ff m b ff d m b

La rochele a xxxiiii. notes a .iiii. mesures
R b ff ddd ff m b ffd m b ff ddd

m b ff d ff m b

ORlyans a xxxvii notes a .iiii. mesures
R b ff ddddd ff m b ff ddd m b ff

d m ddd ff m b ff ddd m b

r r b/ss d [d d d d] r r r b

37. La rochele   In 32̇ notes and 4 measures

R b ss d d d ss r r r b/ss d r r r b/ss

d d d r r r b/ss d ss r r r b

38. Orlyans   In 36̇ notes and 4 measures

R b ss d d d d d ss r r r b/ss d d d r r

r b/ss d ss r r r b/ss d d d r r r b

9. Mamour

In 30 notes and 3 measures

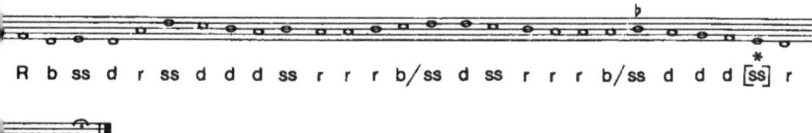

R b ss d r ss d d d ss r r r b/ss d ss r r r b/ss d d d [ss] r

r r b

10. Alenchon

In 30 notes and 4 measures

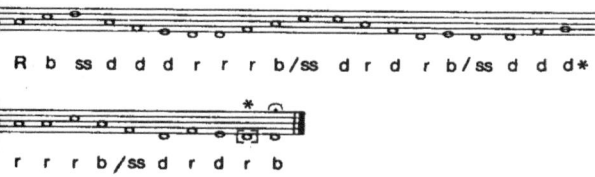

R b ss d d d r r r b/ss d r d r b/ss d d d*

r r r b/ss d r d r b

11. La portingaloyse

In 30 notes and 4 measures

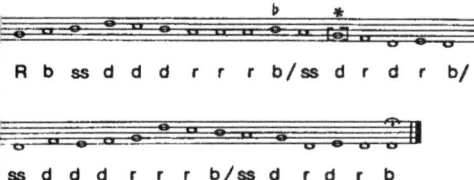

R b ss d d d r r r b/ss d r d r b/

ss d d d r r r b/ss d r d r b

12. Vatem mon amoureux desir

In 39 notes and 4 measures

R b ss d d d ss r r r b/

ss d ss r r r b/ss d d d ss r r r b/ss d r ss d d d ss r r r b

3. Ioyeusement[11]   In 43̇ notes and 5 measures

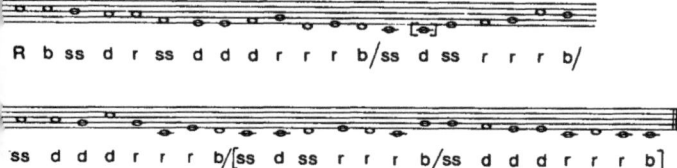

R b ss d r ss d d d r r r b/ss d ss r r r b/

ss d d d r r r b/[ss d ss r r r b/ss d d d r r r b]

4. Passe rose   In 27 notes and 3 measures

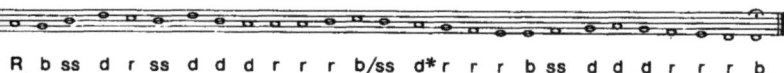

R b ss d r ss d d d r r r b/ss d*r r r b ss d d d r r r b

5. La basine[12]   In 46 notes and 5 measures, and this is played twice.

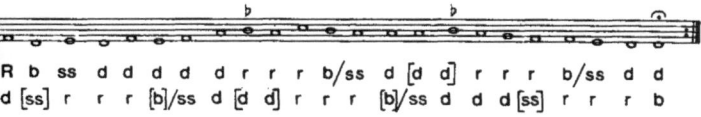

R b ss d d d d d r r r b/ss d [d d] r r r b/ss d d
d [ss] r r r [b]/ss d [d d] r r r [b]/ss d d d [ss] r r r b

6. Ma soverayne   In 39̇ notes and 4 measures

R b ss d r ss d d d ss r r r b/ss d r r r b/ss

1) Two *mesures* are missing from the choreography: I have adopted Jackman's solution (in *Fifteenth Century Basse Dances*) and repeated the second and third *mesures*.

2) This piece is not in B: it is clear where *branles* must be added, but the addition of *pas simples* and *pas doubles* is conjectural.

ſſ ɔɔɔ ſſ ɔ z ſſ ɔɔɔ ɯ b

A marguerite a xxxbiii notes a. b. M
z b ſſ ɔɔɔ ɯ b ſſ ɔ z ɔ z b ſſ ɔɔɔ ɯ b ſſ

ɔ z ɔ z ɯ b ſſ ɔɔɔ ɯ b

V yſes a xxxiii notes. iiii. meſures
z b ſſ ɔɔɔ ſſ ɯ b ſſ ɔ ſſ ɯ ſſ ɔɔɔ ſſ ɯ

b ſſ ɔ ɯ

d d d r̄ r r b/ss d r ss d d d r r r b

7. La marguerite — In 38 notes and 5 measures

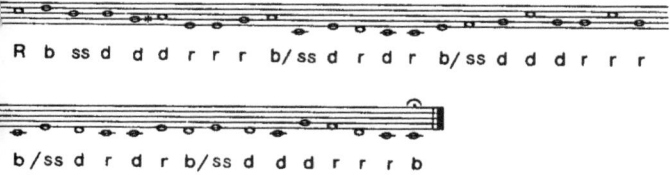

R b ss d d d r r r b/ss d r d r b/ss d d d r r r

b/ss d r d r b/ss d d d r r r b

8. Vyses — In 33 notes and 4 measures

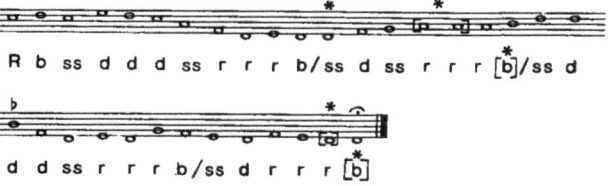

R b ss d d d ss r r r b/ss d ss r r r [b]/ss d

d d ss r r r b/ss d r r r [b]

Cy finissent les regles de dācer toutes dāces auecq̄s celles regles sont notees pour Jouer a tous Instrumens nouuellement īprimees aparis aumont sainct hylaire par Michiel tholouze alenseigne de la corne du cerf

Here end the rules of dancing. All dances according to these rules are written down to be done with all instruments. Newly printed in Paris at Mount Saint Hylaire by Michel Toulouze at the sign of the Hart's Horn.

www.ingramcontent.com/pod-product-compliance
Lightning Source LLC
Chambersburg PA
CBHW040624300426
43661CB00149B/1465/J